Know Abou

Amazing &

Fun Facts with Pictures

By Bandana Ojha

Introduction

Filled with up-to-date information, fascinating & fun facts this book " Know About Kangaroos: Amazing & Interesting Facts with Pictures" is the best book for kids to find out more about the incredible marsupials Kangaroos .This book would definitely satisfy the children's curiosity and help them to understand why Kangaroos are special—and what makes them different from other marsupials .This book gives a story, history, detailed science, explores the interesting and amazing fun facts about kangaroos. It's a fun and fascinating way for young readers to find out more about the world's largest Red Kangaroos, heaviest, Eastern Grey Kangaroos and the smallest Rock wallaby. All about how they got their name, where they live, how the leader male kangaroo dominates the mobs, why and how they fight among themselves, how the female kangaroos take care of her joeys in her pouches up to 12 months- all bits of information which can touch the kid's inquisitive mind. With its awesome facts and action-packed images, this book brings kids close to the lives of kangaroos. This is a great chance for every kid to expand their knowledge about kangaroos and impress family and friends with all "discovered and never known before" fun filled facts.

1. The kangaroo is a marsupial from the family of Macropodidae (macropods -meaning "large foot").

2. The word "kangaroo" derives from the *Guugu Yimithirr* word gangurru, referring to grey kangaroos. The name was first recorded as "kanguru" on 12 July 1770 in an entry in the diary of Sir Joseph Banks.

3. When the first explorer saw one in Australia, he asked a native Aborigine what its name was. Not understanding his question, he said "Kan-Ga-Roo", which is "I don't know" in the Aboriginal language.

I
DON'T
KNOW

Kan-Ga-Roo

4. Kangaroos are the only large animal to use hopping as their primary method of locomotion. Hopping is a fast and energy efficient means of travelling which allows them to cover large distances in habitats where there is little food and water available.

5. Most people think kangaroos are endemic to (live only in) Australia. In fact, several species of kangaroos also live in New Guinea.

6. No matter where you go in Australia, there will be at least one species of kangaroo that lives in and is adapted to that area.

7. The kind of kangaroo found in New Guinea is called a Tree Kangaroo. It looks like a regular kangaroo, except it's very small – about the size of a house cat.

8. The smallest species of kangaroo is known as the rock wallaby and is only about two pounds.

9. There are four species of kangaroo, the Red, Antilopine, Eastern Grey and Western Grey Kangaroo.

10. The red kangaroo, which is the largest and most well-known of all the kangaroo species.

11. Red kangaroo can grow up to 2 meters. They can reach a top speed of over 65km/h – out-pacing a top racehorse. In one leap they can jump 3m high and 7.6m long.

12. The Eastern grey kangaroo is known to be the heaviest species of kangaroo even though the red kangaroo is taller.

13. The adult male Kangaroo is called buck, boomer or jack.

14. Adult female is called doe, flyer or Jill.

15. Young kangaroos are called joeys.

16. Female kangaroos have a pouch called a marsupium in which joey completes its postnatal development.

17. When the joey is born, it is guided safely into the comfy pouch, where it gestates for another 120 to 450 days.

18. Inside the pouch, the joey is protected and can feed by nursing from its mother's nipples.

19. Joeys urinate and defecate in the mother's pouch. The lining of the pouch absorbs some of the mess, but occasionally the mother will need to clean it out, which she does by inserting her long snout into the pouch and using her tongue to remove the contents.

20. The mother kangaroo can suckle two joeys at different developmental stages at the same time with milk that has different nutritional content.

21. Joeys grow quickly, though, and at 14 to 20 months for females or 2 to 4 years for males, they will be fully matured.

22. A female kangaroo can have three babies at the same time: an older joey living outside the pouch but still drinking milk, a young one in the pouch attached to a teat, and an embryo waiting for birth.

23. Kangaroos have small head and small front legs. They are herbivores and regurgitate their food like cows.

24. Kangaroos have good eyesight but only respond to moving objects. sounds.

25. They have excellent hearing and can swivel their large ears in all directions to pick up.

26. All kangaroos have a chambered stomach like cattle and sheep. They regurgitate the vegetation they have eaten, chew it as cud, and then swallow it again for final digestion.

27. Kangaroos can live in almost all types of conditions. They can live in forest, semi-arid environment, and desert.

28. Kangaroos are herbivores. They eat grasses, flowers, leaves, ferns, moss and even insects.

29. The Red kangaroo grazes during the night on a wide variety of grasses and low herbaceous plants, though sometimes this grazing period starts late evening and ends early morning.

30. When water is available it will drink but, if it obtains sufficient green food, it does not need to do so.

31. Western grey kangaroos feed mostly on grass but will browse upon certain native shrubs. They are strictly herbivorous and use microorganisms in the caecum to break down the cellulose of these plants.

32. Kangaroos are essentially the outback version of camels. They need very little water to live and have the remarkable ability to go several months without drinking anything.

33. When kangaroos do finally decide they want something to drink, they like to dig deep holes in the ground to collect rainwater. These little reservoirs continue to provide water for other animals in the area long after the kangaroo has finished drinking.

34. Kangaroos cannot move backwards.

35. A group of kangaroos is called a 'mob', 'troop' or 'court'.

36. The Mobs always have a leader, which is usually the largest male in the group. The leader exerts control over the others with force. He will kick or bite the others into following his lead.

37. Living in mobs can provide protection for some of the weaker members of the group. The size and stability of the mobs vary between geographic regions.

38. Fighting has been described in all species of kangaroos.

39. The kangaroo fights by attacking its opponent with its front paws (which have sharp claws) or by kicking them with its powerful hind legs.

40. Both male and female kangaroos fight for drinking spots, but long, ritualized fighting or "boxing" is largely done by males.

41. During fighting, the combatants adopt a high standing posture and paw at each other's heads, shoulders and chests. They will also lock forearms and wrestle and push each other as well as balance on their tails to kick each other in the abdomens.

42. Winners can push their opponents backwards or down to the ground.

43. These fights may serve to establish dominance hierarchies among males, as winners of fights have been seen to displace their opponent from resting sites later in the day.

44. Dominant males may also pull grass to intimidate subordinates.

45. The large and strong tail is used for balance when hopping, and as fifth limb when moving about on all four legs.

46. "Roos" is a colloquial name used for any kangaroos or wallabies.

47. Western grey kangaroos are very vocal. The mothers communicate to the joeys with a series of clicks.

48. Western grey kangaroo males are known as stinkers due to their strong, curry-like smell.

49. The number of kangaroos in a mob can vary from 3, 4 to 100.

50. Kangaroos don't sweat, instead they lick their front paws and rub the moisture onto their chests to cool down.

51. Kangaroos are adept swimmers, and often flee into waterways if threatened by a predator. If pursued into the water, a kangaroo may use its forepaws to hold the predator underwater to drown it.

52. The average age of a wild kangaroo tends to be less than 10 years, although some kangaroo individuals in the wild have been known to get closer to 20 years old. Kangaroos generally live to about the age of 23 when the kangaroo is in captivity.

53. The female red kangaroo is often called the "blue flyer" because of her blue-grey fur. In the eastern part males are usually red (pale red to brick red) and females a bluish grey, elsewhere, both sexes may be reddish/brown.

54. Kangaroos have also been featured on coins, most notably the five kangaroos on the Australian one-dollar coin.

55. On the Australian coat of arms, the Emu and the Kangaroo were selected as symbols of Australia to represent the country progress because they are always moving forward and never move backwards.

56. The Australian Made logo consists of a golden kangaroo in a green triangle to show that a product is grown or made in Australia.

57. Australian airline Qantas uses a kangaroo as their symbol.

58. The greatest threat to the kangaroo population is human.

59. Most kangaroos are thriving in the wild and doing just fine. But there are many species that are considered threatened, vulnerable, endangered, or critically endangered.

60. Although kangaroos are not commercially farmed, wild kangaroos are often pursued by human hunters for sport, meat and fur.

61. Heat, drought and hunger due to vanishing habitat are amongst the dangers these amazing animals face.

62. Kangaroos are shy and retiring by nature, and in normal circumstances present no threat to humans.

Please check this out:

Our other best-selling books for kids are-

Know about **Sharks**: 100 Amazing Fun Facts with Pictures

Know About **Whales**:100+ Amazing & Interesting Fun Facts with Pictures: " Never known Before "- Whale's facts

Know About **Dinosaurs**: 100 Amazing & Interesting Fun Facts with Pictures

Know About **Kangaroos**: Amazing & Interesting Facts with Pictures

Know About **Penguins**: 100+ Amazing Penguin Facts with Pictures

Know About **Dolphins** :100 Amazing Dolphin Facts with Pictures

Know About **Elephant** :100 Amazing Dolphin Facts with Pictures

All About **New York**: 100+ Amazing Facts with Pictures

All About **New Jersey**: 100+ Amazing Facts with Pictures

All About **Massachusetts**: 100+ Amazing Facts with Pictures

All About **Florida**: 100+ Amazing Facts with Pictures

All About **California**: 100+ Amazing Facts with Pictures

All About **Arizona**: 100+ Amazing Facts with Pictures

All About **Texas**: 100+ Amazing Facts with Pictures

All About **Minnesota**: 100+ Amazing Facts with Pictures

All About **Italy**: 100+ Amazing Facts with Pictures

All About **France**: 100+ Amazing Facts with Pictures

All About **Japan:** 100 Amazing & Interesting Fun Facts

100 Amazing **Quiz Q & A About Penguin**: Never Known Before Penguin Facts

Most Popular **Animal Quiz** book for Kids: 100 amazing animal facts

Quiz Book for Kids: Science, History, Geography, Biology, Computer & Information Technology

English **Grammar** for Kids: Most Easy Way to learn English Grammar

Solar System & Space Science- Quiz for Kids: What You Know About Solar System

English **Grammar Practice** Book for elementary kids: 1000+ Practice Questions with Answers

A to Z of **English Tense**

My First **Fruits**

Printed in Great Britain
by Amazon

43425452R00030